BASIC SKILLS | **HAL LEONARD STUDENT PIANO LIBRARY**

Ear Without Fear

Volume 3

A Comprehensive Ear-Training Program for Musicians

TABLE OF CONTENTS

ISBN 978-0-634-08801-8

HAL•LEONARD
CORPORATION
7777 W. BLUEMOUND RD. P.O. BOX 13819 MILWAUKEE, WI 53213

Visit Hal Leonard Online at
www.halleonard.com

A Note to Students

You will find this series easy to use. To use the books effectively, you will need a pitch pipe or your instrument and a CD player.

Each chapter is divided into smaller sections. This allows you to focus on one section for a short period of time. Working in small sections is more valuable than trying to cover large amounts of material. Learning this way lays a good foundation as you continue to build your skills.

All exercises and dictations may be used repeatedly for additional practice or review. For written exercises, you may either erase your answers or use a separate sheet of paper.

YOUR CD:
- You may access tracks on your CD by moving from smaller numbers up or from larger numbers down. Simply press the track buttons to find the desired track number.

▶▶| • This button will move forward through the CD.

|◀◀ • This button will move backward through the CD. Larger numbers may be easily reached by moving backward from Track 1 while the CD is playing.

- The dictations and exercises are played once. Repeat tracks as many times as necessary to complete each exercise.

YOUR WORKBOOK:

All of the chapters are set up in the same way. Labeled headings appear on the left-hand side of the page. These headings introduce a series of tasks designed to familiarize you with various melodic concepts and patterns.

NEW ELEMENT

New musical concepts will be introduced under this heading. See **NEW ELEMENT** p. 7 for an example.

LISTENING

Under this heading, your CD will provide exercises that will train your ear. Some examples may include exercises in which you will provide answers based on what you hear. The first one is usually done for you so all you have to do is listen. See **LISTENING** p. 8 for an example.

IDENTIFYING

This next heading provides you with exercises on the CD to listen to and new concepts to practice. You will often need to fill in the blanks, providing answers based on what you hear. See **IDENTIFYING** p. 8 for an example.

MATCHING

Under this heading, you will see a series of boxes containing melodic patterns. You will match the pattern you hear on the CD by indicating the corresponding letter in the space provided. See **MATCHING** p. 8 for an example.

DICTATION

This heading contains a series of exercises in which you will write down the melodic patterns that you hear.

On the CD, you will hear each dictation once. Repeat the tracks as often as necessary to complete each exercise. Simply listen the first time, then complete the dictations as instructed. See **DICTATION** p. 9 for an example.

SIGHT-SINGING

This heading provides an opportunity for you to sing, at first sight, a series of pitches notated on the staff. To begin each exercise, you will need to play the first pitch on your instrument or pitch pipe.

It is important to sing the exercises in a range where they sit most comfortably in your voice.

Remember, with the exercises and dictations, accuracy is what counts. Speed will come later.

You and your teacher may want to chart your progress. Keep a log showing the number of times you had to listen to the exercises before you were able to complete them, and how accurately you were able to perform the sight-singing exercises the first time through. See **SIGHT-SINGING** p. 9 for an example.

INTEGRATION

Exercises under this heading introduce a rhythmic component, added to help develop well-rounded listening skills. It is important to begin to hear not only melodic movement, but to hear rhythmic patterns as well. See **INTEGRATION** p. 10 for an example.

We recommend that you use the companion series:

Rhythm Without the Blues

Rhythm Without the Blues is a comprehensive rhythm-training program. Using these two series together will help you to master the dictations and exercises in Volumes 4 and 5 with success.

A Note to Teachers

Ear Without Fear is an innovative program aimed at building a foundation for reading music and developing the skills to perform it accurately.

Ear training demands heightened listening skills that involve hearing and understanding pitch differentiation. Ear training is distinct from rhythm, which is mathematical in structure and employs different neurological pathways. Because both elements are invariably placed together in music training, the result is often frustration and a sense of failure. In this series, these elements are ultimately combined. Volumes 2, 3, 4, and 5 provide exercises that integrate melodic and rhythmic components.

Educators have long known that step-by-step learning is essential. A sense of accomplishment and confidence at each level is the motivating force behind the desire to continue. This series offers demonstrations, listening exercises, sight-singing, and melodic dictations which will help students to reinforce and hone melodic skills.

We have carefully chosen and organized the materials in this book to make the learning process as accessible to students as possible. The Workbook and the CDs are integrated to provide several learning approaches: AURAL, VISUAL, and PRACTICAL. Together, they present a comprehensive, step-by-step learning program for which the student can assume primary responsibility.

The following concepts will be covered in Volume 3:

- introduction of major and natural minor scales

- introduction of the keys of C, G, F, and D major

- introduction of the keys of A, E, D, and B minor

- introduction of the alto and tenor clefs

- introduction of the order of sharps and flats

- introduction of the major and minor 3rd and the perfect 5th

- introduction of major and minor triads

- demonstrations, exercises and dictations covering these areas.

These materials make use of the tonic sol-fa music reading system developed by British educator John Curwen (1816–1880). Tonic sol-fa facilitates pitch recognition and differentiation.

- It provides a prepared curriculum.

- Students can work independently with well-formatted, easily understood exercises.

- Chapters are easily subdivided for appropriately sized weekly assignments.

- Exercises and dictations are readily available for weekly testing and instruction.

- Lesson time is maximized for instrumental instruction, while ensuring that the student is honing musicianship skills.

Students often find the development of essential rhythm and ear-training skills less exciting than learning an instrument, so a reward system may be helpful. Consider implementing one, using some of the following suggestions:

- Encourage students to keep a log outlining the number of sections and exercises completed over the week. They may also want to keep track of how long it takes to complete each exercise. Students' confidence will grow as they begin to see an increase in proficiency and speed.

- Award incentive points for successful completion of sections and increased proficiency. Give prizes and awards based on accumulated points.

It is recommended that students also use the companion series:

Rhythm Without the Blues

Rhythm Without the Blues is a comprehensive rhythm training program that works in tandem with *Ear Without Fear*. Using them together will greatly enhance the ability of the student to master successfully the dictations and exercises contained in each series.

CHAPTER 1

Introduction of *ti*

NEW ELEMENT

Our new note is *ti* above *do*. When *do* = G, *ti* is F♯ and is written on the top line of the treble staff, or the fourth line of the bass staff.

Sol-fa Shorthand

t = ti

t
F♯

t
F♯

When *do* = C, *ti* is B and is written on the third line of the treble staff or in the space above the top line of the bass staff.

t
B

t
B

When *do* = F, *ti* is E and is written in the top space of the treble staff or in the third space of the bass staff.

t
E

t
E

The interval from *do* to *ti* is called a 7th.

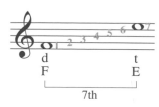

d   t
F   E

7th

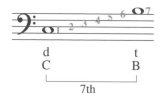

d   t
C   B

7th

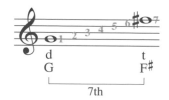

d   t
G   F♯

7th

LISTENING

Listen for the 7th in the following tune.

 PLAY CD TRACK 1

IDENTIFYING

Listen and identify the intervals in the following exercises, then write in the note. Answers are on page 54.

 PLAY CD TRACK 2

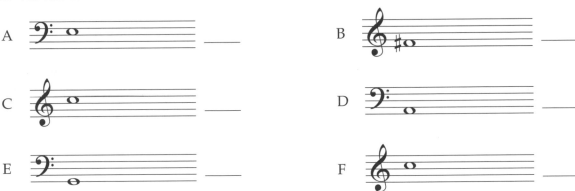

MATCHING

Listen to the tracks one at a time and find the matching tune below. Write the letter of the matching tune in the space provided. Answers are on page 54.

 PLAY CD TRACK 3

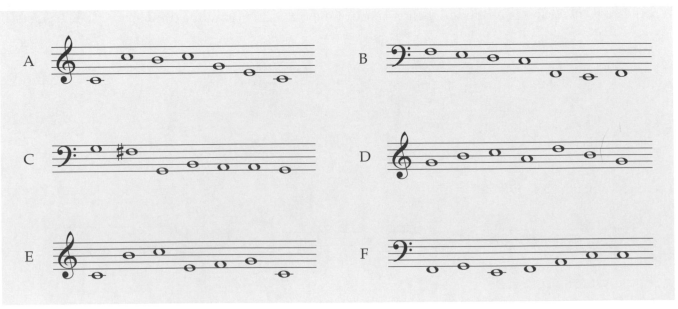

1. _____   2. _____   3. _____   4. _____   5. _____   6. _____

SIGHT-SINGING

For each of the following exercises, play the initial pitch on your instrument or pitch pipe. Sing each exercise twice, once using sol-fa and once using letter names. Check for accuracy on your instrument or pitch pipe.

1.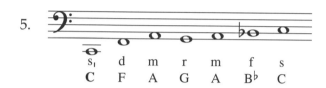

d   t₁   l₁   s₁   d   t₁   d
C   B   A   G   C   B   C

2.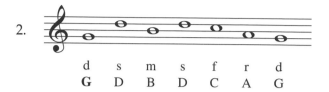

d   s   m   s   f   r   d
G   D   B   D   C   A   G

3.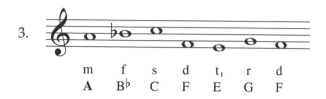

m   f   s   d   t₁   r   d
A   B♭   C   F   E   G   F

4.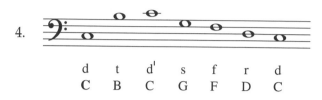

d   t   d'   s   f   r   d
C   B   C   G   F   D   C

5.

s₁   d   m   r   m   f   s
C   F   A   G   A   B♭   C

6.

d   t   l   s   d   s₁   d
G   F♯   E   D   G   D   G

DICTATION

Play the tracks one at a time. Write the melodic pattern that you hear. Answers are on page 54.

 PLAY CD TRACKS 4–5

1.

m ___ ___ ___ ___ ___ ___
A ___ ___ ___ ___ ___ ___

2.

d ___ ___ ___ ___ ___ ___
G ___ ___ ___ ___ ___ ___

3.

s ___ ___ ___ ___ ___ ___
G ___ ___ ___ ___ ___ ___

4.

d ___ ___ ___ ___ ___ ___
G ___ ___ ___ ___ ___ ___

5.

s₁ ___ ___ ___ ___ ___ ___
C ___ ___ ___ ___ ___ ___

6.

d ___ ___ ___ ___ ___ ___
C ___ ___ ___ ___ ___ ___

INTEGRATION

Play the tracks one at a time. Write the melody that you hear.
Answers are on page 54.

 PLAY CD TRACKS 6–9

1.

d

2.

m

3.

s

4.

d

CHAPTER 2

Introduction of tones, major scale, and key signatures C, G, and F major

A **WHOLE STEP** (tone) is made up of two half steps (semitones). Study the examples below on the staff and the piano keyboard.

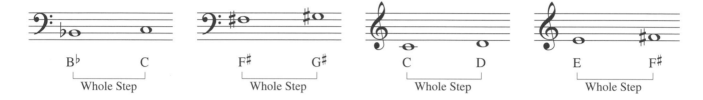

On the piano keyboard, notice that you skip one key, either black or white, to make a whole step.

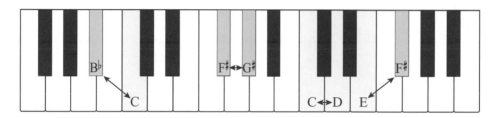

LISTENING

We can hear a number of whole steps in the children's tune, "Mary Had a Little Lamb."

PLAY CD TRACK 10

Whole steps and half steps are used to form musical **SCALES**. The word scale comes from the Latin *scala*, meaning a ladder or steps. A musical scale may be described as a ladder of notes ascending or descending the staff.

A scale is made up of eight notes beginning and ending on the same letter name, arranged alphabetically. Here is an ascending scale where *do* = C.

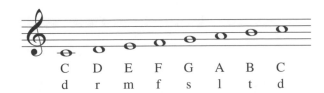

This scale is a MAJOR SCALE. All major scales have the following formula of whole steps and half steps.

Formula for a Major Scale
W W H W W W H

Listen to the C major scale. All major scales have the same tune because they are built using the same formula of whole steps and half steps.

PLAY CD TRACK 11

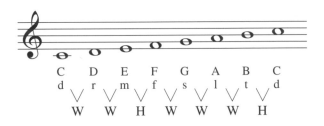

Play the track again and sing along using sol-fa. Listen for the half steps that occur between *mi* and *fa* and between *ti* and *do*.

Let's see how the C major scale and the formula of whole steps and half steps look on the piano keyboard.

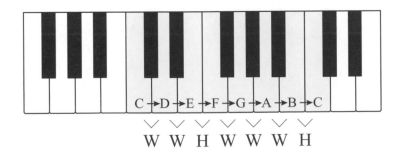

We will now build a major scale where *do* = G. First we write the musical alphabet from G to G.

G   A   B   C   D   E   F   G

LISTENING

Let's listen to what we have so far. Does it have the same tune as the C major scale we heard earlier?

PLAY CD TRACK 12

Play the track again and see if you can identify where the tune goes wrong.

Now we write the formula for a major scale underneath the notes. Then, beginning at the bottom of the scale, we will check each whole step and half step in order to determine exactly where changes need to be made to the pitches to fit the formula.

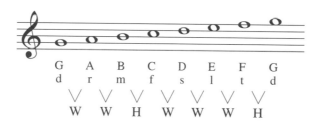

G	A	B	C	D	E	F	G
d	r	m	f	s	l	t	d

W   W   H   W   W   W   H

After comparing all the whole steps and half steps to the formula and checking them with the piano keyboard, we find that the distance between E and F or *la* to *ti* is a half step, but the formula requires a whole step.

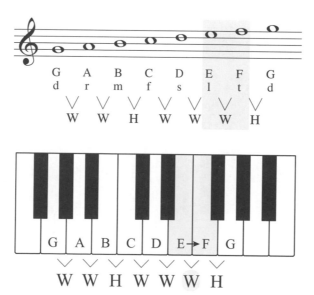

13

In order to fit the formula, we need to raise F by a half step to F♯ to create a whole step up from E.

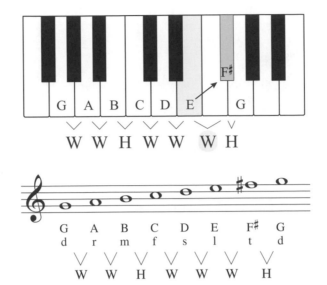

G A B C D E   G
∨ ∨ ∨ ∨ ∨ ∨ ∨
W W H W W W H

G   A   B   C   D   E   F♯   G
d   r   m   f   s   l   t   d
∨   ∨   ∨   ∨   ∨   ∨   ∨
W   W   H   W   W   W   H

LISTENING

Listen to the G major scale. Now we hear the same tune as the C major scale we heard earlier.

PLAY CD TRACK 13

WRITING

Build a scale where *do* = F by adding the musical alphabet, pitches, and formula below. Then complete the scale by adding accidentals where necessary. Answers are on page 54.

Exercise A

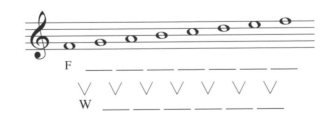

F __ __ __ __ __ __ __
∨ ∨ ∨ ∨ ∨ ∨ ∨
W __ __ __ __ __ __

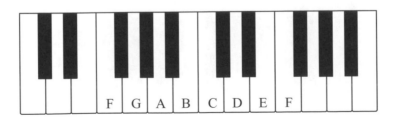

F G A B C D E F

SIGHT-SINGING

Sing each exercise twice, once using sol-fa and once using letter names. Check for accuracy on your instrument or pitch pipe.

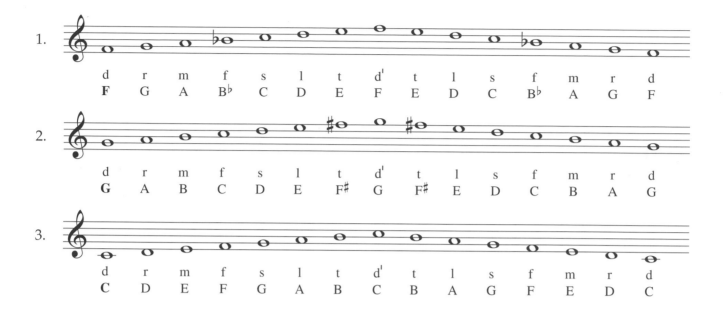

1.

d	r	m	f	s	l	t	d'	t	l	s	f	m	r	d
F	G	A	B♭	C	D	E	F	E	D	C	B♭	A	G	F

2.

d	r	m	f	s	l	t	d'	t	l	s	f	m	r	d
G	A	B	C	D	E	F♯	G	F♯	E	D	C	B	A	G

3.

d	r	m	f	s	l	t	d'	t	l	s	f	m	r	d
C	D	E	F	G	A	B	C	B	A	G	F	E	D	C

So far, we have learned the scales of C, G, and F major. The name of these scales is also the name of the KEY to which they belong. In other words, when *do* = G, we are in the key of G major. When *do* = C, we are in the key of C major and when *do* = F, we are in the key of F major.

When we are in the key of G major, we know that F has a sharp. Instead of writing a sharp in front of every F as it appears in a piece of music, we use a KEY SIGNATURE. For convenience, the sharps or flats necessary for a key are gathered together and placed at the beginning of each staff right after the clef sign.

In G major, to show that all Fs have a sharp, a sharp is placed on the top F line of the treble staff or on the fourth F line of the bass staff, as in the examples below.

In F major, to show that all Bs have a flat, a flat is placed on the third B line of the treble staff, or on the second B line of the bass staff, as in the examples below.

In C major, there are no flats or sharps, so none appear at the beginning of the staves.

*In any given piece of music, it is important to check the key signature before you begin, because the name of the key is also the letter name of **do**.*

WRITING

Write the corresponding key signature at the beginning of each staff. Answers are on page 54.

Exercise B

1.   G major   

2.   F major   

3.   C major   

INTEGRATION

Play the tracks one at a time. Write the melody that you hear. Answers are on page 55.

 PLAY CD TRACKS 14–17

1.
    d

2.
    d'

3.
    d

4.
    s

CHAPTER 3

Introduction of relative minor, natural minor scale, and key of A minor

We have learned the major scales of C, F, and G major, and their key signatures. All major keys have a corresponding RELATIVE MINOR key. Major and minor keys are "related" when they share the same key signature.

To find the relative minor of any major key, go down three half steps from the name of the major key. Using the piano keyboard, let's find the relative minor of C major. Three half steps below C is A.

This shows that A minor is the relative minor of C major.

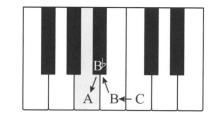

You can also find the relative major of any minor key by going up three half steps from the name of the minor key.

Minor keys also have scales. We will begin with the NATURAL MINOR SCALE. Remember that the formula for a major scale is W W H W W W H. The major scale and its relative natural minor scale share the same pitches and sol-fa, but the natural minor scale begins on *la*. Study the following example.

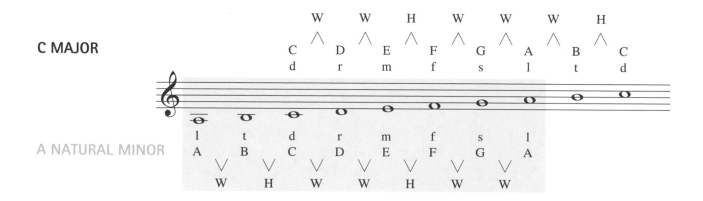

Because the natural minor scale shares the same pitches and sol-fa as its relative major scale, notice that we still have half steps between *mi* to *fa* and *ti* to *do* in the natural minor scale.

LISTENING

Listen to the A natural minor scale.

PLAY CD TRACK 18

All natural minor scales have the same tune because they are built using the following formula of whole steps and half steps.

> ## Formula for a Natural Minor Scale
> ### W H W W H W W

IDENTIFYING

Listen and identify the scales in the following exercises as either major or natural minor, then write in the notes. The first one has been done for you. Answers are on page 55.

PLAY CD TRACK 19

A   major

B   ___

C   ___

D   ___

*In major keys, notes below **do** are indicated with the lower index symbol.*
*In minor keys, notes below **la** are indicated with the lower index symbol.*

MATCHING

Listen to the tracks one at a time and find the matching tune below. Write the letter of the matching tune in the space provided. Answers are on page 55.

PLAY CD TRACK 20

1. _____ 2. _____ 3. _____ 4. _____ 5. _____ 6. _____

SIGHT-SINGING

Sing each exercise twice, once using sol-fa and once using letter names. Check for accuracy on your instrument or pitch pipe.

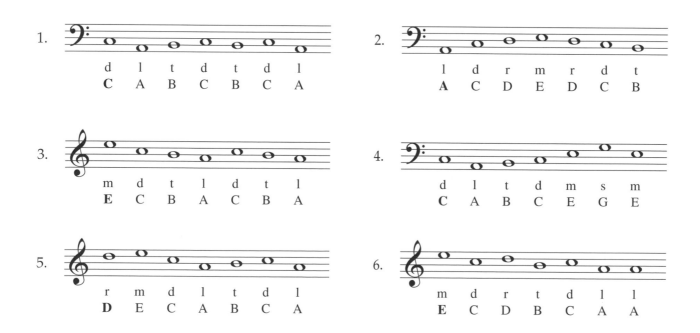

DICTATION

Play the tracks one at a time. Write the melodic pattern that you hear. Answers are on page 55.

 PLAY CD TRACKS 21–22

1.

2.

3.

4.

5.

6.

INTEGRATION

Play the tracks one at a time. Write the melody that you hear. Answers are on page 55.

 PLAY CD TRACKS 23–26

1.

2.

3.

4.

CHAPTER 4

Introduction of the keys E minor and D minor

Using the piano keyboard, we will find the relative minor of G major. Three half steps (semitones) below G is E.

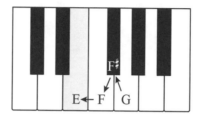

This shows that E minor is the relative minor of G major. We know that the key signature of G major is one sharp: F♯. Since E minor is related to G major, E minor will also have F♯ as its key signature.

We will now build a natural minor scale beginning on E, using the key signature as a guide. First we write the musical alphabet from E to E, remembering to make F sharp.

E F♯ G A B C D E

LISTENING

Let's listen to the scale. We have the same tune as the A natural minor scale we heard in Chapter 3.

PLAY CD TRACK 27

If we write the formula for a natural minor scale underneath, we can see that the F♯ was needed to make a whole step between *la* and *ti*.

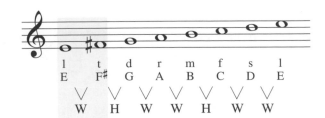

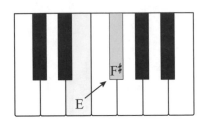

When writing the name of a key, we use the following shorthand to indicate major and minor.

Shorthand

+ = major

- = minor

WRITING

1. **Find the relative minor of F+ and write the key signature on the treble and bass staves below. Answers are on page 56.**

Name of key: _____

2. **Build a natural minor scale in this new key. Begin by adding the musical alphabet and pitches. Then complete the scale by adding accidentals where necessary.**

SIGHT-SINGING

Sing each exercise twice, once using sol-fa and once using letter names. You may want to write in the sol-fa and letter names before you begin. Check for accuracy on your instrument or pitch pipe.

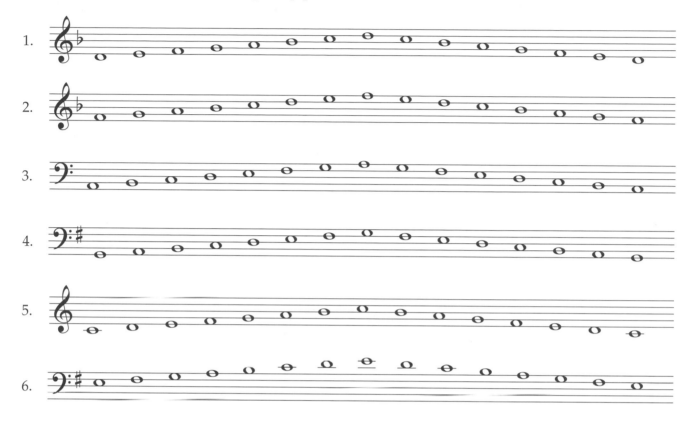

INTEGRATION

Play the tracks one at a time. Write the melody that you hear. Answers are on page 56.

 PLAY CD TRACKS 28–31

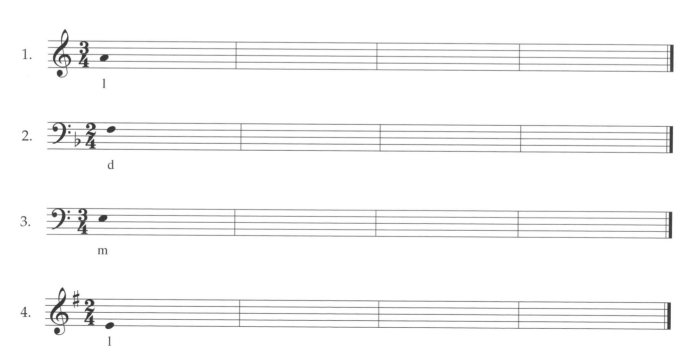

CHAPTER 5

Introduction of +3 and alto clef

NEW ELEMENT

In *Ear Without Fear!* Volumes 1 and 2 we learned to name intervals according to their size; for example, 2nd, 3rd, 5th, etc. Now we will begin to learn to name intervals by their quality as well.

Let's start with the interval of a 3rd. Just as keys are identified as either major or minor, a 3rd can also be identified as major or minor. We will begin with the major 3rd. We use the following interval shorthand to indicate a major 3rd.

Interval Shorthand

+3 = major 3rd

Within the scale, major 3rds occur from *do–mi*, *fa–la* and *so–ti*. Study the examples below in the key of C major.

 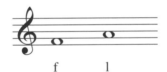 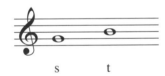

LISTENING

Let's listen to these major 3rds.

 PLAY CD TRACK 32

The familiar tune "Looby Loo" has a number of major 3rds.

 PLAY CD TRACK 33

WRITING

Write major 3rds as indicated on the staves below in the given keys. Use sharps or flats where necessary. Answers are on page 56.

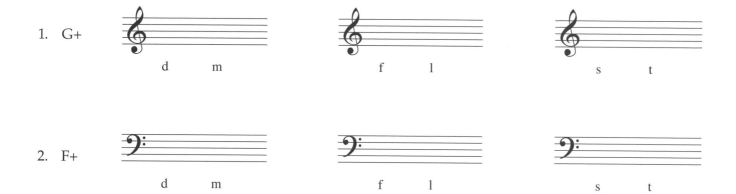

1. G+   d   m   f   l   s   t

2. F+   d   m   f   l   s   t

IDENTIFYING

Listen and identify the intervals in the following exercises and then write in the note. Remember to use the interval shorthand to identify the major 3rds (+3). Answers are on page 56.

 PLAY CD TRACK 34

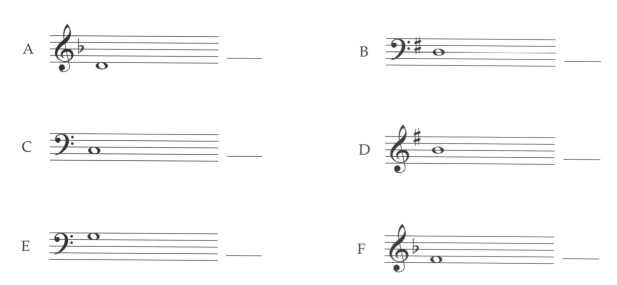

So far we have been using the treble and bass clefs. In this chapter, we will become familiar with the use of the C CLEF. The C clef marks the position of MIDDLE C. Middle C is the first ledger line below the treble staff and the first ledger line above the bass staff, as shown below.

The C clef is used to avoid multiple ledger lines below the treble staff or above the bass staff. There are several types of C clefs. We will begin with the ALTO CLEF. In the alto clef, middle C is marked as the middle line of the staff. Study the example:

Viola music is written in the alto clef. In the alto clef, the key signature for G+ and E- looks like this:

The key signature for F+ and D- looks like this:

WRITING

Write ascending major or natural minor scales in the alto clef in the keys indicated, using the appropriate key signature. Answers are on page 56.

3. A-

4. C+

5. F+

6. E-

MATCHING

Listen to the tracks one at a time and find the matching tune below. Write the letter of the matching tune in the space provided. Answers are on page 57.

PLAY CD TRACK 35

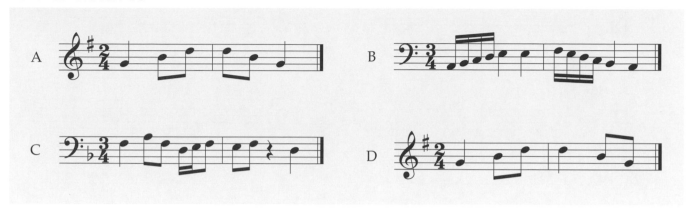

1. _____ 2. _____ 3. _____ 4. _____

Beginning in this chapter, sol-fa will no longer be provided in the sight-singing exercises. However, you may wish to write in the sol-fa for elements that you are less familiar with.

SIGHT-SINGING

Sing each exercise twice, once using sol-fa and once using letter names. Check for accuracy on your instrument or pitch pipe. Rhythm patterns have now been introduced in the sight-singing exercises. As a first step, you may wish to tap out each exercise before performing it.

Remember, it is important to sing the exercises where they sit most comfortably in your voice.

DICTATION

Play the tracks one at a time. Write the melodic patterns that you hear. Answers are on page 57.

 PLAY CD TRACKS 36–37

1.
    m __ __ __ __ __ __
    E __ __ __ __ __ __

2.
    l __ __ __ __ __ __
    D __ __ __ __ __ __

3.
    d __ __ __ __ __ __
    G __ __ __ __ __ __

4.
    d __ __ __ __ __ __
    C __ __ __ __ __ __

5.
    d __ __ __ __ __ __
    G __ __ __ __ __ __

6.
    d __ __ __ __ __ __
    F __ __ __ __ __ __

INTEGRATION

Play the tracks one at a time. Write the melody that you hear. Answers are on page 57.

 PLAY CD TRACKS 38–41

1.
    s

2.
    d

3.
    l

4.
    m

CHAPTER 6

Introduction of P5 and tenor clef

NEW ELEMENT

Certain intervals within the scale are neither major nor minor. These intervals are referred to as PERFECT intervals. Perfect intervals have a pure and open quality. The interval of a 5th is a perfect interval. We use the following interval shorthand to indicate a perfect 5th.

Interval Shorthand

P5 = perfect 5th

Within the scale, perfect 5ths occur from *do–so*, *re–la*, *mi–ti*, *fa–do*, *so–re* and *la–mi*. Study the 5ths below in the key of C major.

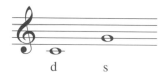

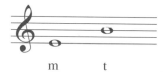

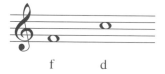

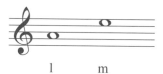

LISTENING

Let's listen to these perfect 5ths.

PLAY CD TRACK 42

"Twinkle, Twinkle, Little Star" shows us a perfect 5th.

PLAY CD TRACK 43

WRITING

Write perfect 5ths as indicated on the staves below in the given keys. Use sharps or flats where necessary. Answers are on page 57.

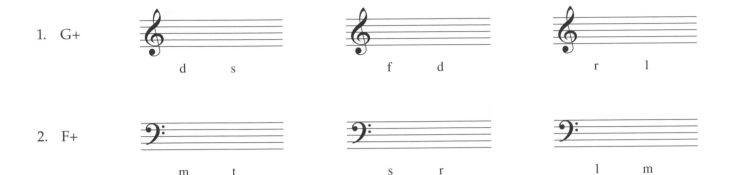

1. G+

    d   s   f   d   r   l

2. F+

    m   t   s   r   l   m

IDENTIFYING

Listen and identify the intervals in the following exercises and then write in the note. Remember to use the interval shorthand to identify the major 3rds (+3) and perfect 5ths (P5). Answers are on page 57.

PLAY CD TRACK 44

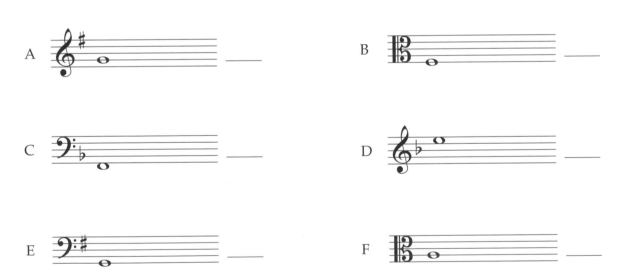

30

In chapter 5, we learned to use the alto clef. Our new clef is also a C clef and is known as the TENOR CLEF. In the tenor clef, middle C is marked as the fourth line of the staff. Study the example:

 ← Middle C

Cello music is sometimes written in the tenor clef. In the tenor clef, the key signature for G+ and E- looks like this:

The key signature for F+ and D- looks like this:

WRITING

Write the ascending major or natural minor scales in the tenor clef in the keys indicated, using the appropriate key signature. Answers are on page 57.

3. F+

4. A-

5. D-

6. G+

MATCHING

Listen to the tracks one at a time and find the matching tune below. Write the letter of the matching tune in the space provided. Answers are on page 57.

 PLAY CD TRACK 45

1. _____   2. _____   3. _____   4. _____

SIGHT-SINGING

Sing each exercise twice, once using sol-fa and once using letter names. Check for accuracy on your instrument or pitch pipe.

DICTATION

Play the tracks one at a time. Write the melodic pattern that you hear.
Answers are on page 58.

 PLAY CD TRACKS 46–47

1.
d — — — — — —
G — — — — — —

2.
d — — — — — —
C — — — — — —

3.
l — — — — — —
E — — — — — —

4.
m — — — — — —
A — — — — — —

5.
l — — — — — —
D — — — — — —

6.
m — — — — — —
E — — — — — —

INTEGRATION

Play the tracks one at a time. Write the melody that you hear.
Answers are on page 58.

 PLAY CD TRACKS 48–51

1.
m

2.
l

3.
d

4.
s

CHAPTER 7

Introduction of major triads, key of D major, and the order of sharps

NEW ELEMENT

A TRIAD **is a group of three notes built in 3rds and sounded together. A triad can be built on any pitch of a scale.**

The pitch the triad is built on is called the ROOT. The second note of the triad is a 3rd up from the root. The third note of the triad is a 5th up from the root. Here is a triad built on G and a triad built on C.

Triads can also be identified by the quality of major or minor. Major triads are built using a +3 from the root and a P5 from the root. Let's look at the major triads built on *do* and *fa*. Study these major triads in the key of F+.

LISTENING

Let's listen to these major triads.

PLAY CD TRACK 52

WRITING

Write major triads as indicated on the staves below in the given keys. Use accidentals where necessary. Answers are on page 58.

1. C+

    s   d
    m   l
    d   f

2. G+

    s   d
    m   l
    d   f

IDENTIFYING

Listen and identify the intervals or triads in the following exercises and then write in the notes. To indicate a major triad, simply write "+ triad." Answers are on page 58.

 PLAY CD TRACK 53

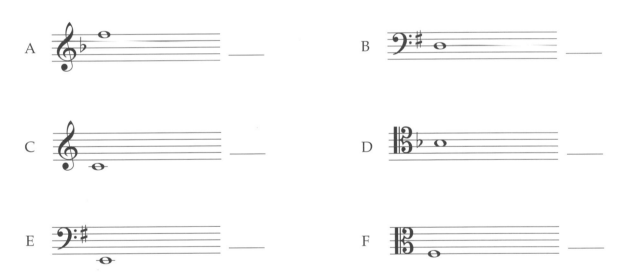

A

B

C

D

E

F

NEW ELEMENT

Our new key is D+. Let's build a major scale in this key. Remember the formula for a major scale?

Formula for a Major Scale
W W H W W W H

WRITING

Begin by filling in the musical alphabet and pitches from D to D on the staff below. Next, write the formula for a major scale underneath the notes. Then, beginning at the bottom of the scale, check each whole step and half step in order to determine exactly where changes need to be made to the pitches to fit the formula. Answers are on page 58.

3.

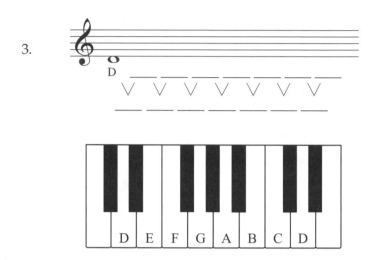

We see that D+ has two sharps, F♯ and C♯. To write the key signature for D+ in the treble clef, we place the F♯ on the top line of the staff. The C♯ is placed in the third space of the staff.

In the bass clef, we place the F♯ on the fourth line of the staff and the C♯ in the second space of the staff.

In the alto clef, we place the F♯ in the fourth space of the staff and the C♯ on the third line of the staff.

In the tenor clef, we place the F♯ on the second line of the staff and the C♯ on the fourth line of the staff.

Some key signatures have more than two sharps. A key signature may contain as many as seven sharps. These sharps always occur in the same order. The order of sharps is as follows.

Order of Sharps

F C G D A E B

An easy way to remember the order of sharps is by using the following sentence. The first letter of each word represents the name of the sharp.

Father **C**harles **G**oes **D**own **A**nd **E**nds **B**attle.

You may wish to create your own sentence to help you remember the order of sharps.

This sentence is a useful tool for determining key signatures. If a scale or key has one sharp, we know that the sharp will be F simply by using the sentence. If a scale or key has two sharps, we know that the sharps will be F and C.

We will continue exploring keys, their corresponding scales, and the placement of sharps as we move through the series.

WRITING

Write the following major triads as indicated in D+, using accidentals where necessary. Answers are on page 58.

4. D+

```
s          d
m          l
d          f
```

LISTENING

Triads can be written and sounded in two ways. SOLID triads are written vertically on the staff and pitches are sounded together as in the example below. Listen to this solid triad.

 PLAY CD TRACK 54

BROKEN triads are written separately on the staff and the pitches are sounded one at a time as in the example below. Listen to this broken triad.

 PLAY CD TRACK 55

MATCHING

Listen to the tracks one at a time and find the matching tune below. Write the letter of the matching tune in the space provided. Answers are on page 58.

PLAY CD TRACK 56

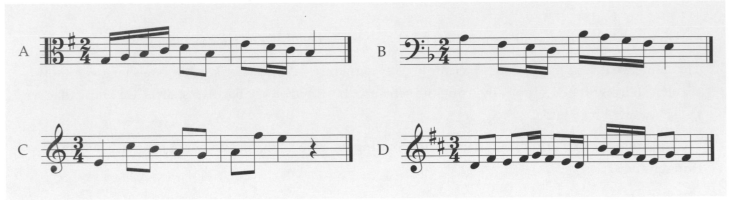

1. _____ 2. _____ 3. _____ 4. _____

SIGHT-SINGING

Sing each exercise twice, once using sol-fa and once using letter names. Check for accuracy on your instrument or pitch pipe.

DICTATION

Play the tracks one at a time. Write the melodic pattern that you hear.
Answers are on page 59.

 PLAY CD TRACKS 57–58

1.

   m _ _ _ _ _ _
   F# _ _ _ _ _ _

2.

   d _ _ _ _ _ _
   D _ _ _ _ _ _

3.

   l _ _ _ _ _ _
   A _ _ _ _ _ _

4.

   s _ _ _ _ _ _
   C _ _ _ _ _ _

5.

   m _ _ _ _ _ _
   F# _ _ _ _ _ _

6.

   m _ _ _ _ _ _
   B _ _ _ _ _ _

INTEGRATION

Play the tracks one at a time. Write the melody that you hear.
Answers are on page 59.

 PLAY CD TRACKS 59–62

1.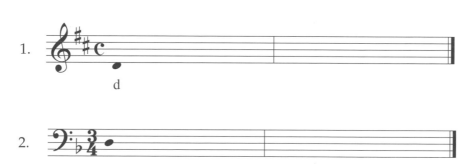

   d

2.

   l

3.

   d

4.

   s

CHAPTER 8

Introduction of -3

NEW ELEMENT

Minor intervals are a half step smaller than major intervals. Let's compare the major 3rd and the minor 3rd examples below.

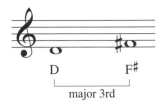 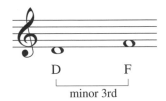

When we take away the sharp from the major 3rd in the first example, we lower the note by a half step and this makes the interval a minor 3rd. We use the following interval shorthand to indicate a minor 3rd.

Interval Shorthand

-3 = minor 3rd

Within the scale, minor 3rds occur from *re–fa*, *mi–so*, *la–do* and *ti–re*. Study the 3rds below in the key of F major.

 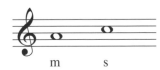 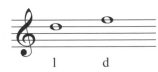 

LISTENING

Let's listen to these minor 3rds.

 PLAY CD TRACK 63

The tune "Rain, Rain, Go Away" has quite a few minor 3rds.

 PLAY CD TRACK 64

WRITING

Write minor 3rds as indicated on the staves below in the given keys. Use sharps or flats where necessary. Answers are on page 59.

1. G+

   m   s   l   d   t   r

2. C+

   r   f   m   s   l   d

IDENTIFYING

Listen and identify the intervals or triads in the following exercises, then write in the notes. Answers are on page 59.

 PLAY CD TRACK 65

A   B

C   D

E   F

41

MATCHING

Listen to the tracks one at a time and find the matching tune below. Write the letter of the matching tune in the space provided. Answers are on page 59.

 PLAY CD TRACK 66

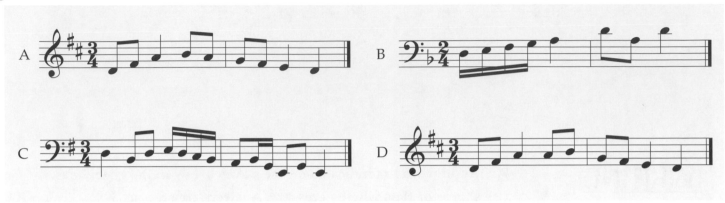

1. _____ 2. _____ 3. _____ 4. _____

SIGHT-SINGING

Sing each exercise twice, once using sol-fa and once using letter names. Check for accuracy on your instrument or pitch pipe.

DICTATION

Play the tracks one at a time. Write the melodic patterns that you hear.
Answers are on page 59.

 PLAY CD TRACKS 67–68

1.

     m __ __ __ __ __ __ __
     A __ __ __ __ __ __ __

2.

     l __ __ __ __ __ __ __
     D __ __ __ __ __ __ __

3.

     m __ __ __ __ __ __ __
     E __ __ __ __ __ __ __

4.

     m __ __ __ __ __ __ __
     B __ __ __ __ __ __ __

5.

     s __ __ __ __ __ __ __
     A __ __ __ __ __ __ __

6.

     s __ __ __ __ __ __ __
     G __ __ __ __ __ __ __

INTEGRATION

Play the tracks one at a time. Write the melody that you hear.
Answers are on page 60.

 PLAY CD TRACKS 69–72

1.

     l

2.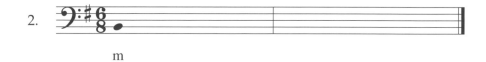

     m

3.

     s

4.

     m

CHAPTER 9

Introduction of minor triads and key of B minor

NEW ELEMENT

Minor triads are built using a -3 from the root and a P5 from the root. Let's look at the minor triads built on *la* and *re*. Study these minor triads in the key of G+.

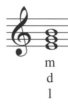

m
d
l

l
f
r

LISTENING

Let's listen to these minor triads.

 PLAY CD TRACK 73

WRITING

Write minor triads as indicated on the staves below in the given keys. Use accidentals where necessary. Answers are on page 60.

1. C+

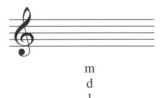

m
d
l

l
f
r

2. F+

m
d
l

l
f
r

IDENTIFYING

Listen and identify the intervals or triads in the following exercises and then write in the notes. To indicate a minor triad, simply write "- triad." Answers are on page 60.

 PLAY CD TRACK 74

A

B

C

D

E

F

1. _____   2. _____   3. _____   4. _____   5. _____   6. _____

NEW ELEMENT

Our new key is B-. Remember how to find the relative major of a minor key to establish the key signature? Go up three half steps from B. You may want to use the keyboard for reference in the writing exercise below.

Now let's build a natural minor scale in the new key. Remember the formula for a natural minor scale?

Formula for a Natural Minor Scale
W H W W H W W

WRITING

Using the key signature as a guide, begin by filling in the musical alphabet and pitches from B to B on the staff below. Next write the formula for a natural minor scale underneath the letter names. Then, beginning at the bottom of the scale, check each whole step and half step to make sure it fits the formula. Answers are on page 60.

3.

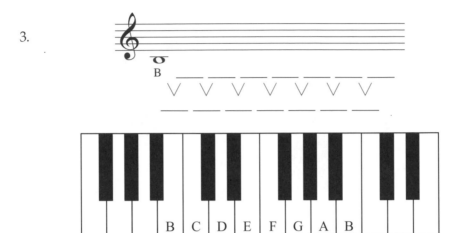

4. Write the key signature for B- on the treble and bass staves.

5. Write the minor triads as indicated in B-, using accidentals where necessary.

m   l
d   f
l   r

46

MATCHING

Listen to the CD and find the matching tunes below. Write the letter of the matching tune in the space provided. Answers are on page 60.

PLAY CD TRACK 75

1. _____ 2. _____ 3. _____ 4. _____

SIGHT–SINGING

Sing each exercise twice, once using sol-fa and once using letter names. Check for accuracy on your instrument or pitch pipe.

DICTATION

Play the tracks one at a time. Write the melodic patterns that you hear. Answers are on page 60.

 PLAY CD TRACKS 76–77

1.

r ___ ___ ___ ___ ___

G ___ ___ ___ ___ ___

2.

l ___ ___ ___ ___ ___

B ___ ___ ___ ___ ___

3.

s ___ ___ ___ ___ ___

D ___ ___ ___ ___ ___

4.

s ___ ___ ___ ___ ___

G ___ ___ ___ ___ ___

5.

m ___ ___ ___ ___ ___

B ___ ___ ___ ___ ___

6.

r ___ ___ ___ ___ ___

E ___ ___ ___ ___ ___

INTEGRATION

Play the tracks one at a time. Write the melody that you hear. Answers are on page 61.

 PLAY CD TRACKS 78–81

1.

s

2.

m

3.

d

4.

d

REVIEW TEST

The test consists of six parts: Review Questions, Matching, Identifying, Sight–Singing, Dictation, and Integration.

Possible points are listed to the left.

Answers are on pages 61–62.

POINTS	

REVIEW QUESTIONS

1   1.   Explain how to find the relative minor of a major key. _____

                _____

1   2.   The interval of a 3rd may have the quality of major or minor. T _____ F _____

2   3.   Draw a tenor clef on the staff: ⎯⎯⎯ Middle C is on which line or space? _____

2   4.   A major triad is built using a _____ and a _____ from the root.

1   5.   How does a minor triad differ from a major triad? _____

12   6.   Write the following triads on the given roots below. Write in the sol-fa and indicate whether each is major (+) or minor (-). Each exercise is worth three points.

           i.   _____   ii.   _____

                   ___   ___

                   ___   ___

           iii.   _____   iv.   _____

8   7.   On the staves below, write scales in the given keys, adding accidentals where necessary. Use whole notes and mark the half steps using this symbol: ⋁

         F+   E-

Each scale is worth four points: one point for writing the scale correctly, one for correct accidentals, and one for the correct positioning of the half step symbols.

8. For the following exercises, write in the appropriate key signature and name the key.

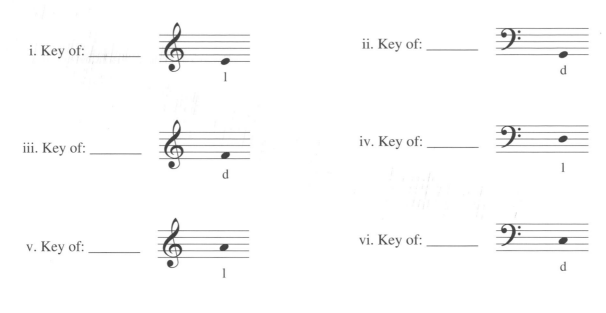

i. Key of: _____   ii. Key of: _____

iii. Key of: _____   iv. Key of: _____

v. Key of: _____   vi. Key of: _____

vii. Key of: _____   viii. Key of: _____

There is a total of 43 points in this section. You should score 39 or more before continuing.

Score: _____ out of 43

MATCHING

Listen to Track 82 and find the matching melodies below. Write the letter of the matching melody in the space provided. Each answer is worth one point, for a total of six points.

🔘 PLAY CD TRACK 82

1. _____   2. _____   3. _____   4. _____   5. _____   6. _____

IDENTIFYING

Listen to Track 83 and identify each triad as either major or minor.

 PLAY CD TRACK 83

1. _____   2. _____   3. _____   4. _____   5. _____   6. _____

SIGHT-SINGING

Sing each exercise twice, once using sol-fa and once using letter names. You may choose to write the missing sol-fa under each exercise. Check for accuracy on your instrument or pitch pipe.

1.

2.

3.

4.

5.

6.

Each accurately sung exercise is worth one point, for a total of 6 points. There is a total of 18 points in this section.

You should score 15 or more before continuing.

Score: _____ out of 18

DICTATION

Play Tracks 84–86. Write the melodic patterns you hear. Each answer is worth six points, for a total of 48 points.

 PLAY CD TRACKS 84–86

1.

2.

3.

4.

5.

6.

7. (alto clef, sharp, whole note)

l ___ ___ ___ ___ ___ ___
E ___ ___ ___ ___ ___ ___

8. (treble clef, flat, whole note)

l₁ ___ ___ ___ ___ ___ ___
D ___ ___ ___ ___ ___ ___

POINTS

INTEGRATION

Play the tracks one at a time. Write the melody that you hear.

PLAY CD TRACKS 87–92

14   1. (treble clef, 2/4)
        l

18   2. (alto clef, 3/4)
        d

21   3. (bass clef, sharp, 3/4)
        d

13   4. (alto clef, flat, 2/4)
        l

16   5. (bass clef, sharp, 2/4)
        s

19   6. (treble clef, flat, 3/4)
        m

149

Score: _____ out of 149

If you have scored a total of 139 out of 149 for the dictation and integration exercises,
Congratulations! You may now move on to

Ear Without Fear! Volume 4

If your score was 138 or less, you should review any elements
that gave you difficulty before continuing.

ANSWERS

CHAPTER 1

IDENTIFYING:

A — ∨ 7th   B — ∧ 2nd   C — ∨ 2nd

D — ∨ 6th   E — ∧ 5th   F — ∨ 4th

MATCHING:

| 1. B | 2. D | 3. C | 4. A | 5. F | 6. E |

DICTATION:

1.
m f s m d t₁ d
A B♭ C A F E F

2.
d t l s m l s
G F# E D B E D

3.
s l s d r t₁ d
G A G C D B C

4.
d t d' s f m d
G F# G D C B G

5.
s₁ t₁ d m f s d
C E F A B♭ C F

6.
d t₁ l₁ s₁ d t₁ d
C B A G C B C

INTEGRATION:

CHAPTER 2

WRITING:

Exercise A

F G A B♭ C D E F
∨ ∨ ∨ ∨ ∨ ∨ ∨
W W H W W W H

Exercise B

1. G major

2. F major

3. C major

INTEGRATION:

1.

2.

3.

4.

CHAPTER 3

LISTENING:

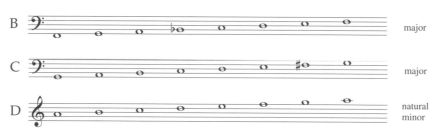

B ...... major

C ...... major

D ...... natural minor

MATCHING:

1. B   2. D   3. C   4. F   5. E   6. A

DICTATION:

1.
l	d	m	f	r	r	m
A	C	E	F	D	D	E

2.
m	r	d	t	l	d	t
E	D	C	B	A	C	B

3.
l	t	d	r	m	s	l'
A	B	C	D	E	G	A

4.
l	m	f	m	d	t	l
A	E	F	E	C	B	A

5.
l	s,	l	t	d	m	s
A	G	A	B	C	E	G

6.
m	r	d	t	l	m,	l
E	D	C	B	A	E	A

INTEGRATION:

1.   2.

3.   4.

CHAPTER 4

WRITING:

1. Name of key: D-

2.
    D E F G A B♭ C D

INTEGRATION:

1.

2.

3.

4.

CHAPTER 5

WRITING:

1.
    d   m   f   l   s   t

2.
    d   m   f   l   s   t

IDENTIFYING:

A   ∧ -3   B   ∨ 5th   C   ∧ 8th

D   ∨ +3   E   ∧ +3   F   ∧ 4th

WRITING:

3.

4.

5.

6.

MATCHING:

1. A   2. D   3. B   4. C

DICTATION:

1. m d s, d r m d
   E C G C D E C

2. l l' s m r d t
   D D C A G F E

3. d l d m l' s l'
   G E G B E D E

4. d l s, f, m, l l
   C A G F E A A

5. d m f l m t d
   G B C E B F♯ G

6. d d' s t d' s d
   F F C E F C F

INTEGRATION:

CHAPTER 6

WRITING:

1. d s   f d   r l
2. m t   s r   l m

IDENTIFYING:

A ∨ 2nd   B ∧ P5   C ∧ 7th
D ∨ +3   E ∧ 4th   F ∨ P5

WRITING:

3.
4.
5.
6.

MATCHING:

1. B   2. C   3. A   4. D

DICTATION:

1.
d s l r d s₁ d
G D E A G D G

2.
d s f d' t s d'
C G F C B G C

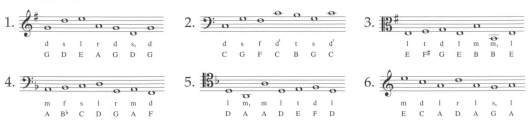

3.
l t d l m m̄₁ l
E F♯ G E B B E

4.
m f s l r m d
A B♭ C D G A F

5.
l m₁ m l t d l
D A A D E F D

6.
m d l r s₁ l
E C A D A G A

INTEGRATION:

1.

2.

3.

4.

CHAPTER 7

WRITING:

1.

2.

IDENTIFYING:

A ∨ P5

B + triad

C ∧ +3

D ∨ 6th

E ∧ 4th

F + triad

WRITING:

3.

D E F♯ G A B C♯ D
∨ ∨ ∨ ∨ ∨ ∨ ∨
W W H W W W H

4.

MATCHING:

1. B   2. C   3. A   4. D

DICTATION:

1.
m s d r m d d
F# A D E F# D D

2.
d m f l d' t d'
D F# G B D C# D

3.
l t d m r f m
A B C E D F E

4.
s t d' l f s d
C E F D Bb C F

5.
m d f m s t d'
F# D G F# A C# D

6.
m r d l t d l
B A G E F# G E

INTEGRATION:

1.

2.

3.

4.

CHAPTER 8

WRITING:

1.

2.

IDENTIFYING:

A   ∨ +3

B   ∧ -3

C   ∨ P5

D   ∧ 6th

E   + triad

F   ∧ 2nd

MATCHING:

1. D   2. C   3. A   4. B

DICATION:

1.
m s f r m d r
A C Bb G A F G

2.
l d d m s m m
D F F A C A A

3.
m d r t m d l
E C D B E C A

4.
m r d l d t l
B A G E G F# E

5.
s m l s m r d
A F# B A F# E D

6.
s d' l f s m d
G C A F G E C

INTEGRATON:

1.
2.
3.
4.

CHAPTER 9

WRITING:

1.
2.

IDENTIFYING:

A — triad   B + triad   C ∨ -3

D ∧ 7th   E ∨ 4th   F ∧ +3

WRITING:

3.

B C# D E F# G A B
W   H W W H W W

4.
5.

MATCHING:

1. C   2. D   3. B   4. A

DICTATION:

1.
r f l l s m d
G B♭ D D C A F

2.
l d r m r d l
B D E F# E D B

3.
s d' t s l f s
D G F# D E C D

4.
s m f r l, t, d
G E F D A B C

5.
m s l' m d r l
B D E B G A E

6.
r l d t l m, l
E B D C# B F# B

INTEGRATION:

1.

2.

3.

4.

QUESTIONS:

1. Go down three half steps from the name of the major key.

2. True

3. C is on the fourth line.

4. +3   P5

5. A minor triad is built using a -3 from the root.

6. i. +   ii. +

   iii. -   iv. -

7.

8. i. Key of: __E-__   ii. Key of: __G+__

   iii. Key of: __F+__   iv. Key of: __D-__

   v. Key of: __A-__   vi. Key of: __C+__

   vii. Key of: __B-__   viii. Key of: __D+__

MATCHING:

1. D   2. F   3. A   4. E   5. B   6. C

IDENTIFYING:

1. +   2. -   3. -   4. +   5. +   6. -

DICTATION:

1.
d s, l, t, d m s
G D E F# G B D

2.
m r m l, s, r d
F# E F# B A E D

3.
l, m f s m d l
B F# G A F# D B

4.
s d t, d s f r
C F E F C B♭ G

5.
d t d' s l t d'
D C# D A B C# D

6.
d s l t d' d m
C G A B C C E

7.
l t d m r r l
E F# G B A A E

8.
l, s, d r s l' f
D C F G C D B♭

INTEGRATION:

Hal Leonard Student Piano Library

A piano method with music to please students, teachers and parents! The **Hal Leonard Student Piano Library** is clear, concise and carefully graded. Perfect for private and group instruction.

Piano Lessons 1-5
Appealing music introduces new concepts

Piano Lessons Instrumental Accompaniments 1-5
Correlated audio CD or General MIDI disk for lessons and games books

Piano Practice Games 1-4
Listening, reading, and improvisation activities correlated with lessons book

Notespeller for Piano 1-3
Note recognition activities

Piano Theory Workbook 1-5
Written theory activities correlated with lessons book

Piano Technique Book 1-5
Etudes to develop physical mastery of the keyboard (Instrumental Accompaniments optional)

Piano Solos 1-5
Additional correlated repertoire (Instrumental Accompaniments optional)

FOR MORE INFORMATION, SEE YOUR LOCAL MUSIC DEALER, OR WRITE TO:

HAL•LEONARD® CORPORATION

7777 W. BLUEMOUND RD. P.O. BOX 13819 MILWAUKEE, WI 53213

Visit us online at **www.halleonard.com/hlspl.jsp**

Book 1
Piano Lessons
Piano Lessons CD
Piano Lessons GM Disk
Piano Practice Games
Piano Technique Book
Piano Technique CD
Piano Technique GM Disk
Piano Theory Workbook
Piano Solos
Piano Solos CD
Piano Solos GM Disk
Notespeller for Piano
Flash Cards Set A

Book 2
Piano Lessons
Piano Lessons CD
Piano Lessons GM Disk
Piano Practice Games
Piano Technique Book
Piano Technique CD
Piano Technique GM Disk
Piano Theory Workbook
Piano Solos
Piano Solos CD
Piano Solos GM Disk
Notespeller for Piano
Flash Cards Set A

Book 3
Piano Lessons
Piano Lessons CD
Piano Lessons GM Disk
Piano Practice Games
Piano Technique Book
Piano Technique CD
Piano Technique GM Disk
Piano Theory Workbook
Piano Solos
Piano Solos CD
Piano Solos GM Disk
Notespeller for Piano
Flash Cards Set B

Book 4
Piano Lessons
Piano Lessons CD
Piano Lessons GM Disk
Piano Practice Games
Piano Technique Book
Piano Technique CD
Piano Technique GM Disk
Piano Theory Workbook
Piano Solos
Piano Solos CD
Piano Solos GM Disk
Flash Cards Set B

Book 5
Piano Lessons
Piano Lessons CD
Piano Lessons GM Disk
Piano Technique Book
Piano Technique CD
Piano Technique GM Disk
Piano Theory Workbook
Piano Solos
Piano Solos CD
Piano Solos GM Disk

Supplementary
Teacher's Guide & Planning Chart
My Music Journal
Flash Cards Set A
Flash Cards Set B

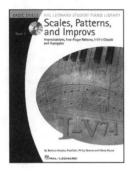